# Rose in the Afternoon
# and othe

Dedications are unfashionable so
To readers for whom thought is food this book is offered

and in gratitude dedicated
To those hospitable spirits whose thought is life, and at whose lavish tables I have been sustained

Among those living J.W.B.
D.A.N.J.

# Rose in the Afternoon and other poems

Jenny Joseph

J. M. Dent & Sons Ltd · London

First published 1974



Printed in Great Britain by
Biddles Ltd, Guildford, Surrey
and bound at the
Aldine Press · Letchworth · Herts
for
J.M. DENT & SONS LTD
Aldine House · Albemarle Street · London



This book is set in 11 on 12 point Press Roman

ISBN 0 460 02162 1

Some of the poems included in this volume have appeared in the following:

*Outposts*
*Tribune*
*The Listener*
*P.E.N.*
*Living Poets*
*Modern Poetry*
*Oxford Book of Twentieth-century English Verse*
*The Times Literary Supplement*
*Encounter*
*New Statesman*
*B.B.C. Radio*
*Time and Tide*

CONTENTS

## TO KEEP EACH OTHER WARM

To keep each other warm; eat
To weight the belly, and like cocoons lie
Wrapped away from the street,
Shifting only for comfort
In a long dozing,
Is understandable in dark, in Winter,
And it is almost proper that Tom, Dick, Harry
Or even Paris,
No more should give to or want from Joan, Liz, Mary
Or even Helen.

But oh what grace or pardon shall we get
If before Winter we hibernate;
If eyes not old but tired stare at the coals
While heaving seas bring down the fish in shoals
About our coasts,
And even the old brown lazy-rolling one
Turns in the pond sluggish with unstirred weeds
To gulp the air
That in its channels myriad movement breeds
But we shut door

Stay close within pretending to be old
Because we cannot bear to face the cold
We know will sweep down through those powerless trees
No country wood but decorative frieze—
They lack protection that can do no harm;
Then soon these walls will stand as square as snow
Whirling before an edgy wind, and so
Neither Tom Dick Harry nor even Paris
Joan Mary Liz nor even Helen could
Be content, and we not even,
Graceless and desperate, keep each other warm.

## WOMEN AT STREATHAM HILL

They stand like monuments or trees, not women,
Heavy and loaded on the common's edge
Pausing before the leaves' decline; far off
The railway runs through grass and bushes where
Slim girls and interested lovers seem
Another species, not just generation:
Butterflies flitting in the leaves, not stones.

Nobody asks what they have done all day
For who asks trees or stones what they have done?
They root, they gather moss, they spread, they are.
The busyness is in the birds about them.
It would seem more removal than volition
If once they were not there when men came home.

Ah giggling creamy beauties, can you think
*You* will withdraw into this private world
Weighted with shopping, spreading hands and feet,
Trunk gnarling, weatherworn? that if you get
All that your being hurls towards, like Daphne
Your sap will rise to nourish other things
Than suppliant arms and hair that glints and beckons?
Your bodies are keyed and spry, yet do you see
*Any*thing clearly through the grass-green haze
Hear anything but the murmur of desires?

Bargains in bags, they separate towards home,
Their talk a breeze that rustles topmost leaves
Tickles the dust in crannies in the rock:
Beetles that grind at roots it touches not.
The women pull their thoughts in, easing like stones
Where they are set, hiding the cavities.
They care as little now to be disturbed
As flighty daughters urgently want peace.

## PRO PORTION

The fall of a sparrow is an easy thing
Or baby thrush with its alarming eye
Hopping in panic on a garden wall.
It needs but cat, or lorry wheel or boot.
And we have built so solid for ourselves:
Our concrete towns above are rooted in
Structures as heavy underneath the earth.
Springs, wires and pulleys, intricate needle points,
Drugs and lights and measurements preserve
Each aspect of our bodies; dentists, physicians,
Upholstery in velvet rooms, specialists,
All the equipment and the many who make it,
Wrap us round with comfort for survival.
And yet how quickly can this fine machine –
This fed, oiled, cared, protected human thing –
Topple, and this precision engine go
Careering down the gully where it lies
In ineffectual havoc, churning stones.

Plants and animals' lives are chanced and wasted:
Haphazard fish that spawn then swim away
Nests in rickety trees, seeds wide open;
While we spend life planning a sure perfection.

For us one wayward ounce can set the pointer
Swinging across the dial face, all broken,
Whereas the sparrow and the sparrow's egg,
Easy crushable things,
Wing off into the sun as strong as glory.

## HOMO SAPIENS

The sun has lost its heat, dahlias
Burn in its stead; brown and tattered leaves
Make way for fruit, at times like a Spring displacement.
Earth's secret mists rise and mesmerise.
The lamps burn violet and the tar in the evening
– As one hears said gunpowder was to horses.

But the cat rolls and stretches, not budging, knowing no danger
And women, gorging in gardens on fruit to ripen
The seed within, loll dishevelled awhile,
More like the cat than watching it.

In beech woods husks lie finished on the ground
The stems grow straight for miles, clothing the slopes.
The ripening kernel does not split the tree.
The old cat in the sun has lost its spring
But has no need to climb out on the tiles
Having had thirteen kittens and lost an eye.
It will die when it is kept no longer.
Our downfall is we must be fruit and flower.
Where flowers are for fruit, a second bloom
In a season is rare. We must be husk and tree
Contrive to stand, as if the tree trunk, split
And empty of sap, still drew its life from the earth,
As if the husk put forth the shoot and leaves.
Flabby bag of bones, what hope is there?
We cannot shed the blained and calloused body
Like a burst peapod lightly dropped on the ground.
So wasteful then this garden . . .

Through the bled body the pale green shoot of the mind,
Breaking the crusted earth – the Autumn flower.

## A KIND OF ANSWER

Window of the soul, they say, the eye.

If, as in some South room on to a garden,
Set about with climbers that smell sweet,
The window is one for seeing into, where
At a round table to the sounds from outside
The occupant sits working, my direct gaze
Is not one; as through an ambulance eyehole,
You'll see nothing that way – the straight stare
Makes the glass blank. But
As well as to be taken in, the soul
Stands to look out,
And feels it sees more in not being seen;
Stares from the darkness so you'll not see past,
Speared in the shafts of light, stands paralyzed.

Yet searching, searching, across all those meadows
For another house with windows that flash open.

## FALSE PREMISE?

Do they do sky-writing any more?
I saw such a swirl in the air, so definite a pattern
(Art Lettering, with the O falling back in the S)
Someone must have put it there;
I watched it stretch, and blur, then it wafted off as clouds do.

If I came to the window now, and, looking down
At the woman pegging a blanket out for the wind,
Only now raised my eyes above the little gardens,
I might think 'that sort of wind shows storm
Somewhere up there, as does the washing leaping.
Remember to put a hat on if you go out.'

Does the chance of a sight so influence intention,
And our understanding of it and of causes—
We have caught or missed it but it was always there—
Or is it among the things that get moved around
Like inert and fettered shirts, filled by a wind
Whose direction is not local and whose force
Is general, not to do with us?

The wind will blow intentions anyway,
But were they there, or did it bring them with it?

## CANCER ART

Watching the children playing by the lake
We looked, no doubt, idyllic. Rosy faces
Ran up to ours as mirror for their joy;
Smiling and calm at apogee we seemed,
But something of our dubbed appearance due
To merely being cover for what's left
Behind; in a chilly unaired house the actual
Tenant fidgets gloomily to pray:
'Noisy and tolerant – oh forgive
Those whose small brain needs quiet, those who
Will squeeze the rashness from you in deadly earnest.
(See on our ride here how I smashed my finger –
The poison ticks like cruelty within);
Forgive the gross demands for what you cannot
Give, what you should not, since in all things natural
You love like that, and we inordinate.
Forgive that in your children's need we offer
Our useless grief at what we do to you.'

This cry alone might save, but that it is
Self-pity's anguish at its paucity.
The roses lose their glisten and the lake
Fades to its real extent – light on a puddle,
The Sunday scene a growth in an airless brain:
The wound's attempt at health providing death.

## A PERSPEX BLOCK – ABOUT 2″ DIAMETER

One of those shores unvisited by the dead;
Unhaunted, rather, by that part of us
We cling to more than to our memories
Of how that beach once was, of what a field
Lay there, where glazed pipes and cables now lurk under
Forecourts to garaged houses –
Anaesthetized by vacuum to the movements
That twist an object and prevent the beam
(Skilled hand to organ, image to image, the same)
Illuminating what we have our mind on –
This little seabed made real by the glass
Sealed from all sustenance, from even what a germ can live on,
One tiny crab, three bits of grit, one leaf,
Is purely what it seems to the outward eye:
A free and calmly watered thriving shore
Unmystified by anything that's actual.

## LANGUAGE TEACHING: NAMING

Why are we frightened of the word for love?
We feast our eyes on eyes that light the soul.
The word is not more perilous than the dreams
We live on, poisoning the system.
We are not frightened of the acts of love.

I walked along an unfamiliar road
And all around, the birds twittered and danced
Through hedgerows blowing in a flat-land wind.
I wished I knew their names and then instead
Of saying 'small, brown, with a spearing beak,
Taking a little run then going back,
Twittering a note that rose to a whistle then sank,
You know, those birds you see in hedgerows
Somewhere along the roads from Hertfordshire'
I could say 'thirp' or whatever bird it was,
And you would know in an instant what they were
How looked, what doing. I'd have caught the birds
In that one word, its name, and all the knowledge
You might have had that I'm not master of
Would straight away be there to help me out.
Naming is power, but now
The birds twitter and dance, change and so escape me.

Why are we frightened of the sound called love?
We talk quite freely about what we need,
We risk enormous punishment when we must.
Is this the word made flesh, rising to grasp us?
You'd think the act made flesh would impinge more
Than a tiny breath made actual through the voice box.
Grammar is power, is witchcraft, is enchantment.
Droplets and air rise from our lungs like a genie
Twisting huge from a bottle to fill a room.
Say 'love' not 'like' (changing tight voiceless sounds
Only a little to get that deep voiced 'v')
The iron gate clangs behind you, and beyond
The bridge in flames, swamps and no road ahead.
We only stay alive on what the word means
So why are we frightened of the name of love?

## WARNING

When I am an old woman I shall wear purple
With a red hat which doesn't go, and doesn't suit me.
And I shall spend my pension on brandy and summer gloves
And satin sandals, and say we've no money for butter.
I shall sit down on the pavement when I'm tired
And gobble up samples in shops and press alarm bells
And run my stick along the public railings
And make up for the sobriety of my youth.
I shall go out in my slippers in the rain
And pick the flowers in other people's gardens
And learn to spit.

You can wear terrible shirts and grow more fat
And eat three pounds of sausages at a go
Or only bread and pickle for a week
And hoard pens and pencils and beermats and things in boxes.

But now we must have clothes that keep us dry
And pay our rent and not swear in the street
And set a good example for the children.
We must have friends to dinner and read the papers.

But maybe I ought to practise a little now?
So people who know me are not too shocked and surprised
When suddenly I am old, and start to wear purple.

## AN EXILE IN DEVON

Deep in English country lanes I walk
'Herb Robert' she says 'and that's Red Campion.
We have White Campion too, but it's not so common.
Round this bend we suddenly see the sea
And – yes there it is. Almost a Cornish blue.'

I listen to her chatter like a chant
One does not hear the words of. Young and free
She never has known greater danger than
All who watch tides and storms in a peaceful country.
Her two fair children grow where there is room
To learn the names of butterflies and flowers.

Though partly I pray that she may stay like this,
Something in me would like to see her lips
Twisted in sadness, like to see her ugly,
Stumbling to problems that are none of hers.
Her complete niceness makes me very lonely.
If I could smash that fairness she could know me,
If I could make her hate, I could make her live.

Excited with a child's regardless glee
'Oh look at the sails' she cries 'a Spinnaker'.
Here in this haven of peace and Campion,
Herb Robert, wild strawberries, seas of a Cornish blue
I ache for the misery that I fight against.
These fresh free children and green land are none of mine.

## OLD MAN GOING

I do not much mind what happens to me when you have done.
I remember my mother making herself miserable
Saving for a decent funeral.
Death isn't ever decent, and dying's the last thing you know.
I'm sure of that now, watching a stray fly
Crawling over the great far space of thick
Cream gloss paint so high above my head.

I don't mind what you do with the bits when I'm dead.
When you take off this ruddy drip and fold up the tubes
And wheel away the catheter, for the last time Thank God,
And let my stinking body rot in its uraemia
There will not be any of it I want honoured.

Mind you *I* wouldn't want anyone's bits and pieces
But if someone else wants to live like that, they're welcome
To use anything of mine; then again
If you're too old to live you can't pass anything on.

My cousin, of course, she would be shocked to hear me.
She'll see to it all, she's done it for all my brothers.
She'd want to think it made a difference to me.
But it's while I live I want a bit of honour.
My last wishes I won't know about
It's the last but one or two I want respected.

I used to sit on the Green on sunny days.
Which direction would it be I wonder?
Of course even if I knew I could never get there now.
And the women flaunted past, trit-trot, trit-trot.

If only one of them had looked
With something of the look they have when they think they
can use you,
When they size up the young beef and estimate what they
could do with this or that one.

That's what I used to mind. All their moments
Riddled with calculations about the next one,
They tugged away their children. *They* would have stopped,
Unconcerned with consequence; but the grown ones think
'If I speak to him now, and he's here again to-morrow . . .'

I know I'm going on, and you're wondering
If I've got a point to come to, but the nurse'll come soon
And I'm coming to it soon, but what I used to think
About the girls that passed was, they could spare one minute
For a real look and word from all the years
And years and years of minutes they had left.
'What you in such a hurry for?' I wanted to say
'Tripping towards old age?'
                                        I wanted to ask them –
But they'd have taken it amiss. The young are touchy
Not the little 'uns, mind, but the married women.

When I was in that life, I was bitter sometimes
Not having some of it, but now
I'd give you anything to have one hour
One full hour warmed right through my skin by the sun.
Pretty women would go by, and children and dogs,
And I'd bask in the light that shone from their filled round skin
And my heart would warm me, moved by their muscles' tension.
I wouldn't moralize or mind the litter,
I'd feed on it all; life round me would give me breath,
Not the dead air supplied by your pumping engine.

One hour, knowingly.

I went there once, on a very damp day, in the evening;
I don't know why, I just wanted somewhere to go
And I thought of the Green; when I got there it was empty.
The fine rain put at a distance the noise of the town.
Swept and clean it looked; much larger: empty.
Slowly, very slowly, across the space through the grey
I saw a man coming, it seemed from the far corner.
I don't remember he ever came up, though I waited.
The sun would mean nothing to me now. I'd feel uncomfortable
Sitting, disgusting, in all that light. Now
If I think of the Green, I see that grey man coming.

## INSIDE HOUSES

1.
Tender of time the solitary stares
Half out of door, clinging to the jamb
As if to shelter, who is never assailed
By any greeting.

'Not now', and 'not this' his shrinking cries,
Mouthed silently, to those who never threaten
To come, to interrupt, to swallow the other possibilities

That someone may come, may interrupt, may arrive, may
occupy, may love.

2.
Slack lower lip trembling like a bee-stung cheek
The old crone says, when she feels she stands too long
For moving people to find reasonable
'Waiting for my daughter.'
'Silly old thing' is the most the neighbours say
'She knows no one could possibly believe, after all these years
Of waiting for her daughter, that she expects her.
Why doesn't she get out a bit and see real people?
There's Mrs Porritt over the way, older than her,
No stronger, anyhow, and she gets out.'

Not that she would mind missing the daughter;
But how could she afford, so meagrely evented,
To miss the knowledge she'd been visited?
Of late she's found relief. The gasman called.
Sudden resource to lighten these empty days:
'Got to wait in in case the gasman calls';
Timely defence against the need for daughters.

## REDISTRIBUTION

They sat on the polished floor and ate up the huge orange
He had left for his wife.
They got the skin off with his special spring screwdriver
Rusting it, although a fruit knife
Lay in its place in the drawer. On sheets of paper,
Cream linen, kept in a box for the fairest of fair copies
They scribbled little notes and added up,
And used, to unblock a drain
A slender silver pencil he had gone to great trouble to get
Engraved with her name.
Allowing this misuse of her prized possessions
Gave her a sense of freedom – no hoarder she
Of having been fondly thought of in retrospect.
They ripped through the velvet substance he had gathered
With such gloomy care
And walked out guffawing and loving into the sunshine,
leaving the French windows
To bang and shatter in any storm that came.

# THOUGHTS ON OXFORD STREET FROM PROVENCE AND ELSEWHERE

Prologue

The doves flap upwards and the fountains play.
Listen to what I'm going to say.
It's to be said out loud in a great voice
Unashamed, unrepentant.
To that small constant voice distracting me
With 'Aren't you being a fool? Is it wise?
Are you sure that's *exactly* what you mean?'
To my constant companion, little whisper, in a great bawl I shout
'Go away'.

I shall not hide behind a personage
Though legend and symbol embarrass less.
I shall not politely suggest 'Take it or leave it'
I offer no choice.
I shan't be modest, and my style won't please
By smoothness or brightness or wit. I care little now
That the clever should think me sane, the well-turned-out praise me
The mighty bless.

I care little, even, that I talk so much about myself.
We all talk about ourselves. What bores
Is the man in vacuum drooling on and on.
Myself includes another person like you –
You fat woman, overloaded, hot, grumbling;
You, blind beggar not entirely blind;
You, small child who have lost your cat
And wail, and wail; and even you, little cat
Licking your paws in another household.
I am more than myself because I want to know you.

And anyway, I do not see that you should listen less to me
Than to someone else who has less to say.

To those who have got this far, I ask this.
Give us a little trust, be generous,
Don't scorn us because we shall never show
In all its glory the sun rise, the crammed earth
In all its fullness mined; shall never explain
Exactly what bells do to the stomach when
They clang at evening in a little town;
Why the heart rises with the escalator
To throng among the crowd (for who knows
Who might be coming or going, who might stop and speak –
The road to Damascus: Paddington 5 a.m. on a wet morning?)

No vision worth having can be held in words.
I care about words, but mind more about life.
I chip and chip at the rock but only flakes
Fall off on to the path: the great stone stands
Blocking the passage; though I beat and beat
Flailing with words and gestures I cannot pass
What I know across that stone. You must trust
What lies beyond the stone in each man's eyes;

And you must not abuse
The trust I have in you that you understand me.

You dumb beasts,
Huddling within mist before the sun strikes
Fire from your steaming backs; waiting by fences, dumb beasts
Staring through mist that clears slowly from valleys,
Slowly from wool and fur, all you dumb beasts
Are not so dumb as is my heart to move
To the simplicities of love.
Stone, amassed by grain on grain of sand
Stamped hard, no sun splits nor small rain softens.

But even my heart is not as dumb as these
Spreading in plastic phalanx in the street
Slow-moving herd, a slouching, paper-bagged
Backbone of England.
No echo sounds
From the blocked cavern of my helpless thought
But from those black and solid tombs, no shout.

Through Kent I come from coastal fog to where
The busy blackness thickens to a solid,
Urging to its boiling centre – London.
Into London creep I in the train
Past fire-lit fleece of sheep than whom more dumb,
Heavy with dumbness, I go to find my way.

The road is hard
I'm a dirty old man
I shan't reform and
I don't wish to be
An example for your moralising
I'm a dirty old man and I shan't be anything else
If I can help it.
The road is hard, and it always will be.
If you've nothing for me
Don't waste my time
I've nothing to say
I don't wish to be
An example for your philosophising.
Don't waste my time thinking that I think
That you're of any interest –
Don't waste my time – if you've fucking nothing for me.

You had to wince!
But did you think
I'd talk pretty and
Be genteel?
You don't expect people like me to be genteel do you?
The road is not
And I'm not
And I fucking well shan't be, not
If I can help it.

You don't expect me to respond do you?
For seven years I've been alone
Two would have finished you.
The rain cements my shoes to me.
The dustbins furnish meals for me.
Why wasn't anyone interested seven years ago
Before I became a character and stank?

I would have talked to you then, and glad of it
Grateful for interest even without sixpence.
Had one foot in the grave, respectability, then
And all my mind to it.
Not now.
Not after seeing it all from the park benches,
Not after this blessed easy silence.

You can't want anything of me
Everyone's done me down, I've nothing left
For any man to want. In hospital
They take away your clothes,
Yes, from a poor old man, those well-fed bitches, they
took away me boots.

Leave me
To go my way,
Left alone all day, then.
They always leave me.
I can't talk nice to people any more.
Nice, huh!
The road is not
And I'm not
And I fucking well shan't be, not
If I can help it.

Give us the price of a cup of tea, then
Just a cup of tea, lady, for a poor old man
God bless you lady, make a poor old man's day bright
With a little kindness.
Aw, the silly soft bitch:
The road is not
And I'm not
And I fucking well shan't be, not
If I can help it.

We can love the beggar. The trickster, the criminal layer that frauds and cheats, and kills its enemies, can be pardoned, along with children who cry for what they want. They become colour for novels; it is a gratification for men, wise in the ways of the world, to have knowledge of a secret society that their nicer wives can admire them for – not near enough to feel the boredom, see the discoloured whites of eyes. The vigorous rogue is a stage character

> We will not exile the funny man who sings
> And we know we must have mercy on the damned.

The well-worn sins we know how to recognise and have found a way, one way or another, of converting within the pale. We have found an annexe to contain them, have worked a way out of the dilemma: 'these must be included/there's no place.' And besides, there's historic precedence we can adapt, though one often feels that The Wicked our saints dealt with were marvels compared to the morons to-day: they seemed to be normal men, but bad, people you could talk to, who had sinned, and at least they repented. They didn't just say 'Gerch' and stare.

> But as I say we know they must be included
> And a way has been found, more or less, some one way,
> some another.

Dirt also we have learnt to overcome and say
You shall not hate him for his running sores.
The deformed man that turns the stomach sick
Is human and must not be abandoned. We dare not,
Delicate of mind, say to a man, you stink.
We value man across his dirt; our stomachs
Are controlled by our minds in horrible slums, and our minds
Are kindly; make effort where there is laughter,
Something to be saved, appetite, something to remind us
Of men who swam a sea for an hour of love,
Gorki's men, downtrodden, who danced all night,
Small beaten boys who flourished into giants
By willing it and caring. Those who'll not trouble
To take the car across the street, or smile
Across a fence, unless it comes to get them,
Admire with sighs more immoderate men than they.

But can you forgive someone for not being your image of what you can forgive, a man who has no interest in you? Having condoned on grounds of 'Life' and 'Vigour' can you accept dullness or surliness in sin? The beggar who does not challenge you because you have no fear of wanting what he flies in the face of, the loud children because while you turn your head aching for rest and graciousness you still can say: 'Ah pretty living things – the tomb is silent' – these, yes. But the man who threatens what you really want, belittling your capital whatever it may be, the man who ignores you; can you accept the man who accepts you neither at your own estimate nor his? Can you forgive the man for whom forgiving you is an irrelevancy, who doesn't fling your understanding back in your face, but just lets it lie there, like a sad failed pudding in the road? Can you play a game if there not only are no rules, but no one to play with?

Two by two the policemen go
Down the streets of Soho
There is nothing behind these doors
You and I don't know.

Two by two the policemen go
Down the streets of Soho
There is nothing we don't know
On this well-worn scene.

Stagily the actors go
Down the streets of Soho
We know all there is to know
*We* know what they mean.

Watching from behind a window
Painted backdrop of Soho
There's no inside broadcast secret
You and I don't know.

Wink and nod and drop eyes low
In the green rooms of Soho
Let your crafty silence show
*You* know what they've seen.

Move two steps from the village, go
To Oxford Street where winds blow
Dust over bemacked crowds, know
There is nothing that you know.

Raise the stage-set you have painted
Around anywhere you go,
There is nobody to type-cast
There is nothing that you know.

Two by two the policmen go
Down the streets of Soho
What goes on behind each make-up
You and I will never know.

There I was, sitting in a bar
Newspaper spread, drink beside me
Fine summer evening coming in
Along comes this fellow, gets a drink beside him
Newspaper spread, takes a look around him
'Excuse me' he said (what on earth's coming
He looks so nervous) 'That's all right mate'
'Excuse me but what do you think of the state of the theatre?'

Well, I ask you. No, I mean
What should I think of the state of the theatre?
'It's all right, I suppose, for them that can afford it.'
'But you afford a bet or two, a meal out, a car
A fridge, a tv, a dog and drinks when you want them?'
I don't know what he thought that had to do with the theatre.

There I was, sitting in a bar
Considering what to place, finishing me drink,
Making it last before Jack came –
Interrupting me peace, no tip to offer
Just worritting me for answers and opinions
Along comes this man 'Excuse me' he says
'For troubling your quiet. I'm doing a piece
On the state of the theatre.' 'A journalist? Well,
That's different' I said. He took it all down
All what I told him about what I thought
About the state of the theatre. Opinions are free.
He had to write something. What he thinks I think
Won't hurt anyone. Me? the theatre?
Why should I go to the theatre?

I praised Lord Luck for praising me
The God of Love for loving me
In fur and diamonds trotted I
Down to a London square
A warmly wrapped lady.

The wind swept all the passers on:
To leathered desks dark-coated men
To basement mirrors office girls,
In paste and nylon trotted
Prinked prepared ladies.

The wind swept leaves and colour out
The workmen closed their little hut
All London seemed like a desert
Inside my warmth I tired
Leisured unaiming lady.

And suddenly around the square
Appeared a battered dull brown pair
Man and woman once perhaps,
In street-length garb, with string
A hand-cart hauled.

Around the square as if the wind
Wrapped them away, they did not mind
The buildings, largeness, wealth and style
They hardly seemed to see
So other were they.

They plodded on around the square
Like bits of earth the wind pushed there
Peasant and brown with scratchy string
Knotted round hand, man driving
Donkey woman; so vanished.

From my fur glove I took my hand
White warm and soft with its diamond
Under my hat I felt my ear
Peeping from lacquered hair
Atop well-kept body.

I saw no buildings in the square
None of the lush show rooms were there
Nor model flowers. Behind them washed
A cold colourless sea
And a cold tired lady.

The rain comes down and I wish
My tears could come down with it
Spatter and soften the stone.
The shop blinds drip
The gutters run; the August trees are sodden and hang weeping.
And my heart weeps, would cry out loud for these sodden
beasts
These patient wet feet flapping to and fro
But all I do is glare out at the rain
Dumb and sodden, compassionate but dumb.

How often, oh how often have we said
No more tears, no more talking of August:
The rose may flower and fall but we will not mention it;
Will jump up and shout for joy
At least get up and shout?
But the rain and its habits
And the rose with its life, both falling in damp gardens,
Ignore our resolutions to avoid
Pitfalls that careful minds have watched for us.
It is not rose or rain that is banal.
We will not stop our minds from grooving dully
Ignoring what we know.
We must not weep nor take the rose for symbol
Yet here in my room the pane is lashed and wet
And there are flowers, and the rose petals fall.

The voices I have borrowed to deliver
'What I mean' safely across 'what I say'
Are of no use, and yet my own is hampered.
The large red moon seems very near to-night:
We do not stretch our fingers out to touch it
Yet it stays there and goes on seeming near.
I cannot serve you on a plate to taste
The music from the pub that sounds across
The summer breeze, and yet it fills the evening.
How can words do what the heart cannot?

Heavy dumb and loaded is the mind
Pulled with the loaded tube trains as they go
Deep in the earth, carrying their cargo.
The clumsy feet shuffle and flap, bearing
Not wicked heads but dim; only the powerless
Are innocent, and they are dumb, and so
The fog shuts down; we cannot cross the stone.

So where is all the shouting and the fuss
What were you going to shout about, was there
Any real matter, where has it dissolved to,
Was it just air bubbling through empty water?
Fountains against a wine-dark glass, how you confuse us!

Great river Rhône whose coiling ropy currents
Pull at my memory, by whose distent shores
All this seemed clear – not easy but straight path –
Behind the walled-up failure was a flash.
We cannot keep aloft the falling sparks
To lift the heart, but still inside the rock,
The core of will, the obstinate I am,
Mutters 'You cannot utterly reduce me'.
This pocket of air can split the stone outwards.
There was an arrogant glory there, a power;
Behind the dumbness, somewhere a speaking voice.

## CATCH

Thinking not much of fish, idly at evening
The fisherman casts; heading for sea, swimming,
Casual it takes the bait, sideways, passing.

The fish chokes, pulls; the fisherman engages,
Puts all his play into this sudden catch,
With twice too much for supper can't let go.

Surprised he lands the extra fish and keeps it
Safe in a land-locked pool, where big it grows:
The only tides that move there in its eyes.

## THE SUN HAS BURST THE SKY

The sun has burst the sky
Because I love you
And the river its banks.

The sea laps the great rocks
Because I love you
And takes no heed of the moon dragging it away
And saying coldly 'Constancy is not for you'.

The blackbird fills the air
Because I love you
With Spring and lawns and shadows falling on lawns.

The people walk in the street and laugh
I love you
And far down the river ships sound their hooters
Crazy with joy because I love you.

## EVEN OVER THE FLAT LAND

Over the flat land the clouds go
Puffy white, scudding, in the blue spring breeze,
And birds whirl past, raking their shadows over
Bushes and banks and brooks and gravel stretches:
Tillable open land, with few surprises.

The mountain stands, the weather is born from it.
The purity and strength of the dark tarns
Renew the streams that fructify the plains
But secret, at a distance; the hidden plot
Mysterious like a garden walled, blooms flowers
Perhaps once five years, unaccountably.
The unnamed birdsong glories from the rock.

The mountain stood and summoned, with its shadow
Creeping back valleys, pulling the sunlight in.
'This favoured place,' its buried voices said,
'Is liquor of life to you, and you know it.
You may not really look at me for years
But I stand here, I am, and in your being
My basalt glitters and my brackens root.
And you leave for the plains at your own peril.'

But even over the flat lands the clouds go
And birds, though tame, sing by the chattering water.
Sun and showers stipple the varied land
And I leave for the plains at my own peril,
Creep back into the light of common day
And to your arms, my so undemon lover.

## BRIDE TO GROOM

For this ring upon my finger
You take the finger.
With the finger you have the hand
And all the Winters it was cold as a child;
With the hand you take the arm
And all it has encircled and supported
That now encircles you.
With the arm the shoulder, and the ache in it;
The neck, stiff, and of a stiff-necked people,
And the soft white throat and the hands that have caressed it.

On the neck this head and its thick hair
And under this thick hair the troublous thoughts
The mind that will not let be, nor let you be,
Woven and packed full of twenty-eight years
Which have this day for zenith as one summary.
And with your hand beneath my breast you take
The pumping heart that will not let me be,
And bangs to the sound of traffic, and the ships,
To deaths, arisings, blindness and betrayals
And will not hood the eyes to tell them morning
Is present in the nightmare, or day the dark,
Yet louder than the trumpets says 'I will'
Over the grey and curdling negatives
Rattling before us in the midday sun.
This day we take each other's past and all things
Hateful and marvellous mounting to this moment,
The point of the pyramid on which you slip
This ring to hold
The broad base, and all our future in it.

## THE OVERBOLD

Trapeze artists we
Our only net our humanity.
Each hold or leap on which depend our lives
We try now for the first time in the air.
Amateur we improvise where
Only perfected expertise survives.

They say that teeth
Timing, balance or breath
Are not the weaknesses that let you down
But that the beam, travelling from eye to eye,
Like star above a shipwreck holds you high:

Looking in your eyes I drown, I drown.

## HERE LIES TREASURE: HERE BE MONSTERS

A child looked in the pool
Where last Winter underneath the ice
He'd seen the duck eggs and white pebbles shining.
His eager hand went straight, but, as if blinded
The water clouded and only mud and slime
Grasped his fingers. The pond's grey creature
Swirled in the weed and shivered up his arm.

The mud stirs easily across your face.
The precious stones I surely saw there once
Cloud into useless flint; the guardian monster
Shuts down all access and makes sour the land.

The child would not have nursed his long intent
Had there been nothing there to lure possession.
Without a clay loaded with goods perhaps
No jealous spite would bother to be there
And we could dredge the clear but empty water
Or leave the place, since nothing kept us here.

## NON-COMMUNICANT

A wide river flowed outside our door
Bringing in trees fathoms-high over tarmac.
'Keep the door shut, you can't possibly get over.'
'Where is the river, and what trees?' you said.

All night long the rain and wind upon
The town trapped tight within the occupants.
All night we watched and talked, and then again
'I'll just go out for a short walk' you said.

Seeing no differences you waded through
The shore of rubbish brought against our stairs.
Lack of goodbye was the last I had of you.
'Why, there is no flood at all' your drowned voice said.

## CERTAIN WEATHERS

They say love is a great heat.
In these high hot days, then, let us consider the land:
The peony bursts and the sun draws off its colour,
Great unwinking light, morning and evening, lies on either hand;
Iron in the sky sucks moisture from under concrete,
Day after day the noon blares 'Here I stand'.

And love, they say, is like a roaring wind
Reversing the grasses; lain low they reveal
Their white uncommon underside; it lashes
The lake's back to an edge scraping a scar in the bank that
        will never heal.
The animal rages across the country, it is
A wind, like Orpheus, to make the trees kneel.

Then the tired cooling comes, and in the town
Sapless lies wreckage that the winds brought down.

But no one says that love is changeable
The start-stop rain that has us all in doubt;
A sun enough only to bring out flies;
Wind that pushes our hopes scudding from the horizon, now
        promise now wash-out;
Front line forever lost: as finally
Enemy melted – no victory, no rout.

Underground stalks fill as the rain seeps in
The earth withstands the drought and hurricane.

## ZENITH

The enormous heat has encircled the garden
Raising our boundaries a hedge-height in a week.
Distraction of birds has slacked the string that held
Our actions steady, pace by pace along.
We stand suspended. If we move we fall.
Then we are back and prone upon a cliff–
The mist from the world's cataracts bemusing.
Now we are only a surface for sun, like fruit:
Later, we say, later the purposes.

Perhaps our happiness is like this summer:
Holding, corrupting, laying on the air
A sweet narcotic, making the plums fall
Squelchy, ripe, tasteless when they lie too long.

Men though, more than oranges, can store
The sucking heat of love, and oh what Autumns
Active and calm, should our stunned selves provide,
Full of the God, drunk; like Danaë with gold?

## NO MAP AVAILABLE

We turned and waved, arms raised above our load,
To those still fretting up the border slope:
'We've got our loot through, see you on the road
If you're as clever', turning to exult
(Aware, a little, that we would remember
This glee, the cluster of guards thwarted, and the valley withdrawi
More than stuff smuggled to cheer us through November)
We missed the minute we could still get free in.
We stood and gestured, and the weather struck.
We trudged back to the bottom for another day.

Simply, what had lain ahead was the very worst
We had ever travelled through, or survived, and our joy,
Whirled away by a wind we thought we knew,
Was no help. To have the proper equipment
Was what we needed, or not to go that way.

Nor will this do.
                                        As map or record of
That unreliable country we inhabit
It is about as true
                                        As the Old Sarum Hitler bombed, to England.
For you
                    have come not separate recognized roads with me
But through the marshes seeped your influence.

These sort of stories serve to circumscribe a truth
And lasso an isolatable adventure that has gone,
Tying it into a pattern—mountain, plain, storm. (Enthusiasts
At rest in the evening enjoy inching their way with string
Over the map they have walked) but we
Can't make a foray *into* time (getting trophies, marking routes):
We are clad in it and it moves with us.
You cannot really view the air you breathe,
The egg is nourished from within its sphere.
To organise a symbol for the living
That is you and me wearing our every day,
I would have to wrench rhythm, ignore sense, say
We are the air we breathe, we, following
Our path, are the paths we walk upon.

## A VERSION OF THE PHOENIX STORY

A bird flew down from a tall tree
Into my hands, and settling there
Said 'Shelter me

'And I will tell you of woods where
You can listen to the bark grow,
To the loom weaving the air,

'And when I am strong we will both go,
You on my back, to places that otherwise
You could not know.'

The bird slept and I waited
My hands tied for fear of letting it fall.

When it woke it bristled and became fierce
Pecking and clawing at my wrist and arms
So that I opened my hands after all.

As with a scream it plummeted
'You have betrayed me,' the bird said.
'Yes, but you made me,' I answered.

## AN ANIMAL STORY

In those days, you know, we had a house with a big garden
Currant bushes, strawberry nets, wild daffodils, nursery beds,
the lot–
Land on three sides up to the next large garden
And at the bottom fields, then tangled woods.

I remember very clearly one Summer evening
Late enough for the heat to have gone out of the sun
Late for us to be up,
This little stranger quite petrified on the lawn
In the middle of a large shaven space and a ring of people
Further from cover than it had ever been.

We were charmed that we could keep the baby rabbit.
We had wanted a rabbit and here one had just landed
And there was no alternative but to let us look after it.
I am sure we took great care.
I am sure we packed it with lettuce leaves
Tried to keep it warm
Anxiously moving its box wherever we went
For fear some cat might get it.

All I remember is our first delight
In finding it dropped on our path
And the sight that, when I think of it these days, appals my
mind still:
How in the morning all that furry body
Pushed against the sides of the shoe box
Larger in death than he had seemed at first,
The rabbit we had saved.

The grown-ups around us were loving and thoughtful people.
Can it be that they hadn't actually known?
Were they dressing to go out, or how did it happen
They didn't tell us the things we needed to know
To prevent us killing the rabbit that we loved?

## FABLES

i

The gentleman that my black hen lays eggs for
Has diamond links joining impeccable cuffs
And a suit and a voice and a smile of exquisite finish,
But has never been known to express a liking for eggs –
Which is all that my black hen can lay for him.

ii

The butterfly is dainty flippant fragile
Like the petal it lands on without moving, while
Man is strong, and marvellous in conquest.

Butterflies cross oceans without fuss
Flitting over arid waters; for us
Even to say 'alas' we need trumpets.

iii

This nut withering on the shelf
Enfolds leaves which could contain
Lithe branches, home for singing birds;
Breezes blowing aloft, moist root.

It blackens like an old man's face.
Oh where is the soil and the sweet water
To ease from the crippling shell the shoot?

This small withered nut my brain.

iv

To achieve knowledge, salting away Faust's stock –
Is that better than a certain sort of look
Attained to make another's hackles rise?

Except that the body dies; the body dies.

### v Jack and the beanstalk

The boy planted a bean
Plunging his whole hand with it into the earth
Which he was young enough almost to want to eat.
His mother, engrossed with the years, lolled by the shed
Getting out the washing in a practised slovenly way.
The boy dug deep, like his father, and the bean grew,
Planted for his loud-mouthed mother as his father did.
In the water-green leaves' reflection the child and the woman
Laughed in their fecund world,
His shadow contained within her larger darkness.
Incredible that this soft shadow of his mother
Will soon be a lean man gobbling up fat women.

### vi The blue lagoon

The two young men were warned. They had been told
The blue lagoon was treacherous, that beneath
Its picture-postcard surface lay quicksands.

The frame of bright green trees rises steeply
From water that they longed to flail their arms in
The unscarred strip of silver sand looked firm.

The wood keeps off the noise from the road above:
Their muffled cries were held within that rim.

Visiting children were told this as a lesson
But the youths became heroes we dreamt we would have saved
Had we been there. However, except in dreams
We never would have gone into the wood even
That circled harmlessly, in case some Thing
Caught us and dragged us to the Blue Lagoon.

But later much more arrogant than this
Not satisfied with having what we know
Can never be more safely ours, we must

Pitch ourselves in. When dragging currents take us
What comfort to the bodies as they drown
To say to the water spiders 'We were told so'?

## vii Cutting off one's ears for someone else is wrong

A man paid 110,000 guineas for Van Gogh's mother.
Not even for the woman that breathed, but a picture of her.
If he'd met her when she was what she was
I don't suppose he'd have given as much to her.

And if he had chanced to meet him would he have felt like
  supplying
The painter, even with enough sausage for the rest of his
  natural?
He probably wouldn't have wanted him in his house:
An ordinary functioning man, sleeping and glaring about him.

And although he has to pretend to value her
Saying he'd give his eye teeth or at least his worldly wealth
  to save her,
I daresay he wouldn't really have wanted to give all that money
To have his own mother sitting permanently on his sofa.

A dog would rather have another dog
Than a flat board;

And is just a dog.

## viii Muse

A great bird is swooping over our yard.
Let her have the chickens while she's mine.
We will do without eggs for many a long day.
Looking into the light to see what bird,
She throws blindness like a rag in my eyes.
On all the air, now black, outline of wings
Is clamped like a sizzling horseshoe, like Mercury
Running into itself wherever I look –
The dark fire that neither heats nor lightens.

ix

Stay close, little tortoise, dig in.
Put on the coffee pot fourteen times a day
Day and night intermingled with much slow pottering.
Put your nose out rarely

So that in the Spring
There will be someone calm to note the spot
Where my beautiful friend the hare
Died galloping across the frozen hills.
Stay close, little tortoise, stay alive,
Collect your strength, drip, drip, through months, in a phial,
To sing a dirge for our beautiful friend the hare.

x

Fifty-thousand cats cross our garden –
No, of course not so many, but a quantity you can't count.
They are gross and dirty scavengers and disturb the night like
babies.

What weather is brewing away in those foreign skies?
For suddenly looking at me through the window
Is this long-haired fluffy grey tiny cat never before
Seen, gazing at me out of a white ruff.
A prize-cat, no doubt, strayed in our mongrel yard.
She gazes sweetly and turns, unsure, away.

xi

Think of the minute amount a mouse eats.
The sticky handles of knives will keep them going
Or the bits of grit from a crack in a biscuit.
Really he takes nothing from you.
Insects build colonies from the side of jars
Where the jam has dripped and dried.
Many people think they only take
Things not used up or needed by rightful owners.
What is one smile a week and a kindly thought?
But think what inroads and depradations
A mouse can make. He can gnaw through a wall in a week.
In the end he uses up everything
One ruinous mouthful out of twenty precious books.
He renews his nestful of needs every five weeks.
Think of the eyeless citadels of the ants
Growing as high as trees where no tree grows.
All will be taken after that first nibble.

xii

The washing is jerked from shade into the sun
And the rope half-hitched round the cleat in the same swift
movement.
In the well of the yard stands a woman whose huge haunches
Swivel on solid pillars. Her feet do not move.
Her hands can reach to everything she needs.
A band of sun paints the air by the third floor windows.
She has hoisted the dancing socks from dark to light:
O woman, could you haul me to grace with your strong
right arm?

## GETTING UP IN WINTER

The dark is in my throat
Damp in my brain
The ice holds down time's leg
No fire burns.

Limbs uncoil their ache
Tea loosens pain
Gradually the oil drips through
And the earth turns.

## DIARY

**Dec. 3rd Frost**

The frost is beautiful
But it corrodes;
It splits up mountains,
It hurts the heart.

**Dec. 4th Fog**

The blanket fog
Shuts safe within
The wild ark waters
Whirl unseen.

**Dec. 5th Fog and Frost**

Fog's limpet hand
Holds hard the frost;
Beauty corrodes
Its work unseen.

**Dec. 6th Again**

The grimes of the world
Suffuse the heart:
Creeping, non-combatant
But visibly brought.

**Dec. 7th Finish**

Suddenly, distance
And buildings are there,
Sun washes colour
Through vanishing air.

## FIRST SPRING DAWN

Apples in the garden of Eden
Must have looked like this:
Red and still hanging when other fruit had fallen.
These in a deserted garden
Rebellion or disease
Seem, now we have imposed the seasons.

But all the birds in Paradise
Could not sound like this
First single soaring voice between two dreams;
Out of the whitening sky,
Winding through sleep, singing:
'Spring now is better than all Eden then.'

## THE WRECK

Like Autumn leaves, aimless but appointed
The wreckage sways through layers of water to where
Sea bottom's scavengers have piled their fire
A heatless glory of amber, brown and gold
Glinting through a twilit silent world.

No clankings, screams or roaring of explosion
Echo in these white-floored caverns where
Ship's ruin sends, three days delayed, the ore
For the sea creatures fashioning, the world
Derelict and useless is their glory and gold.

O fisher dreaming on the oil-bound water
That you can share the salvage from this loss
Or in that silence you would suffer less –
Drowned, you could take no interest in that gold:
You must catch fish to catch fish in your world.

## HARD CORE

This island is rock now,
Even the pebbles scraped away by the tides.
Once they had planned to build a little harbour
Or at the least a landing for day trippers
To make me into an amenity
Surrounded by the pleasurable sea.

Whether anything would have come of it, I don't know–
Pleasant the thought of children on my shore
(There would have been shores)
Civilized, cultivated even, connected to the green land,
The water between us clear and sunlit, rippled,
Safe for boys in boats, warming, fish full.
This soft fortune would have befallen me
Brought in on its currents by my friend the sea.

How should I know what happened? Some say
The tides shifted; or that those who liked me
On the city council left, or had other projects
Thrust upon them. The visitors needed a car park;
A couple drowned on their way out to climb me,
Dragged away by the enemy, the sea.

All that was years ago, and laughable really.
I get much compensation from the birds
Passing over to the bread-lined shores
And orange-peel and muck; the icy current
Keeps off most forms of fish, but there are insects.
Water weed chokes the only Southern inlet.
A few still know my name, but most ignore me
Kept distant by my enemy the sea.

But when the winter savages the coast
Men, going down in little boats, scream in the wind
And one large wave discredits a wholc town
Spoiling all its velvets, setting at nought
Its years of hoeing paths, of making clean.
Stripped long ago, I shall be here when even
Marks of their destruction are gone for
There is nothing to sustain me
Save
My beloved enemy, the sea.

## EXORCISM

No master I but able seaman
Moving for money over the world's waters.

The dark wall high beside the wharf proclaimed
'I am the Lord thy God' in Salvation letters.

I did not go to the clean godly hostel
But I looked, as the posters said, for my own salvation.

It happened that I walked upon the hill
That overhung the quay, a quarter entirely
Packed with little grey houses in long grey rows
A hill of brick and asphalt not of grass.

I found friends in a half-demolished house
Playing cards by a candle stuck in a tin.
I would not say that this became my home
But every time we came into the port
I visited the hill and every time
My ship passed down that coast far out at sea
I looked for the pinprick lights, inconstant winking
Quite different from the beacons of the Sound.
I thought I could tell where those four men were sitting.

One day I called and there were brand new houses
Lighted roads with green edges, a clean woman
Cooking in her own kitchen; a garage; gardens.

As we weighed anchor in a freshening dawn
I pulled my own out of my memories.

Over the years I found for my free hours
A doss in other towns, my homing thoughts
Aimed at another cote. We fished elsewhere.

There was a storm once as towards that channel
We steamed our way. Pitch black the decks awash.
Numb with fatigue and years of passing on
I, man at helm but no skilled mariner,
Saw suburb street-lights through the wooded hill.
It saved a shipwreck. Now my clean cool mind
No unhoused vision holds. I wish all well
Within those houses, for there is no pull
To make me cross the road to reach them now
Who once braved tides and captains to do so.

## THE ROAD FROM GLASTONBURY

The holy thorn of Glastonbury sprouted in this dark time
Nearly two thousand years. Spring petals
Float like snow on to the iron cold ground.
They say if you pick a bit when the bush is flowering
It will guard you against all the evils that come.

Bled cold of my fighting strength I turned
Into the Glastonbury road to try my luck.
The action itself warmed me. Cold
And beautiful the Winter sun came up.
Thorns that grew thick as my arm hedged
My view of the approaches.
I huddled and went on.

As I went down the hill I thought I saw
Blossom sway high out of reach, above
A little stunted tree knee-deep in grass.

But maybe it was the snow falling, or the strange light
That snow brings with it, deceiving my sight.
And like the world above the snow, how black
How black and empty the road away from faith.
And then I heard the snarling of the evils
Which thought of the marvellous tree had guarded earlier,
Close by the ditches, just out of sight in the dark
They would lollop with ease beside every inch of that track.

Faith and hope gone left only bleary love
Staggering about in the unhealthy wind.

## AN OLD DREAM BY GRACE REVERSED

It is a long while since I have depended on dreams
Feeding, latterly, instead on fantasies, potions
That sicken the digestion, weakening the limbs.
But the other night I had a dream
Of such sharpness, such real substance as used to supply my days
As an underground stream feeds a denatured field.

I was in the garden I grew up in.
The hedge we used to hide under, a cavern
Floored with dry leaves dropped from the masking holly,
This hedge was of bush roses in the dream.
On one of the sprouting tendrils, by one handle
The other pointing down to the ground, hung
The garden scissors, rusty.

That was all – no people, no events, no memories
Except it was the same place and the same garden:
Beautiful, peaceful, completely quiet: and yet
It was a dream of utter hopelessness.
I woke with my heart wrenched, and my stomach
Sank into the actuality of my day:
A day, a time, a life of hopelessness.
I thought the dream presaged my real loss
But by some grace this difference I found
On seeing you in life who had formed my dream
The dread proved the unreal part, your love was whole.

## DAWN WALKERS

Anxious eyes loom down the damp-black streets
Pale staring girls who are walking away hard
From beds where love went wrong or died or turned away,
Treading their misery beneath another day
Stamping to work into another morning.

In all our youths there must have been some time
When the cold dark has stiffened up the wind
But suddenly, like a sail stiffening with wind,
Carried the vessel on, stretching the ropes, glad of it.

But listen to this now: this I saw one morning.
I saw a young man running, for a bus I thought,
Needing to catch it on this murky morning
Dodging the people crowding to work or shopping early.
And all heads stopped and turned to see how he ran
To see would he make it, the beautiful strong young man.
Then I noticed a girl running after, calling out 'John'.
He must have left his sandwiches I thought.
But she screamed 'John wait'. He heard her and ran faster,
Using his muscled legs and studded boots.
We knew she'd never reach him. 'Listen to me John.
Only once more' she cried. 'For the last time, John, please wait,
please listen.'
He gained the corner in a spurt and she
Sobbing and hopping with her red hair loose
(Made way for by the respectful audience)
Followed on after, but not to catch him now.
Only that there was nothing left to do.

The street closed in and went on with its day.
A worn old man standing in the heat from the baker's
Said 'Surely to God the bastard could have waited'.

## LIGHTHOUSE

The winter sunshine dies around the house
The clock ticks louder in the unlit room
And every knick-knack ornament and plant
Gulps down the dusk and holds the dark more solid.
The shift in the grate of whitening coals is all
That stirs in the private room behind the shop.

Stillest of all the little phial of glass
Enclosing against corruption the white lighthouse
Powdered with snow that has not moved for years.
The son who brought it home is dead long since.
Sunk deep in the leather, what trick in my head
(Or tension in the air beyond my eyes?)
Twirled the sky painted there so that on all
That coast and desolate rocks the snow fell down
Hiding the lighthouse in its purity?

## KITE

I took a kite, not mine, up
To the edge of the town. High
It jerked, bounding
Against the tether which I clung to, knowing
A second's lessening of panic would lose it to me.

Then it steadied, and as it lay on the air
The breath came back into my body. Up there
It floated, and lilted as I turned my wrist.
I felt my movement held the kite to me.

It steadied and my mind moved
Safe once up there
In that blue circle, held within its edge,
Riding at anchor, calm as the kite's riding,
On top of the tugging now, holding the world.

The kite seems mine now, but –
The cord snatched through my palm and
Oh, here I go, up into it and
Help, now I can't let go, won't, because –
                                                  But oh,
Where is the safe sphere I was gazing at
That one blue?
That place complete to the view
Is now the air I breathe.
Gulping I cannot see it.
Countless slivers of light beat round my eyes,

And the eye of the kite, staring above, not helping.

## BONFIRE

An hour or two till dusk with the wind fallen
We lit the fire, collecting all the junk
That over the months had soddened into the corners.
We swept the yard of crumpled leaves and sweet papers
Dusty and rotting.

'That'll never catch, all that damp soggy stuff
And the stench will be awful.'

Suddenly there shot up a flame
Very bright and clear through the coiling rolls
Of oily smoke, and it seemed to burn up the smoke;
Bright, inimitable, worth it.

Then as unaccountably it died.

Ash is everywhere.
Now it is dark
And none of this black ruin will light again.

## MIRROR, MIRROR

At a certain point every morning
I look in the mirror and see a fair country,
And if the sun strikes the wall
I see a face full of strength and interest
That raises its eyes, and nods 'see you later, see you later.'

And as the morning bustles past
I think mainly of getting to that glass,
To a time when I can let my eyes
Linger along the paths that go curving through that country.
And to this end I go swinging through the morning.

At a certain point in the afternoon
I am led far away from that clear place.
Its busyness is shut up, unmarked; between the glass
And where I am turning, dust and vapour revolve
Obscuring the stairway so there seems no access
To such a remote chamber,
But I imagine the country dissolving,
The towers blurring in the mirror as the light shifts.

At a certain point every evening
I walk up the stairs
Open the door
And stand before the mirror
At last, think I, to revisit
My stored, my cherished, my secret country.

But the sun has gone from behind me
And all there is to be seen
Is a flat place where, one would feel, the air stifles.
It turns out to be a tired sagged face
Mouth surly shut, and whose somewhat ashamed eyes
Glare downwards refusing to utter even 'Alas'.

In a certain small hour
On the occasions when I wake looking for to-morrow,
A gleam flickers through the glass again.
The sketch of a face brushes across the rectangle
Whispering 'to-day, to-day' as it passes.

One day
And it could be any next day
The glass will stay blank.

## TO A FRIEND, DEAD IN AFRICA

A Sunday Winter mist lies on London
And through it little groups of chimney stacks
Spiral their slow smoke: this roof-top scene
Would be a stage-set or quaint picture in
The country where you died – land where the sun
Draws scorching dazzle even from an icy sea,
Paints red the hot rock, dries and makes sharp the grass.

Perhaps one day little irregular houses
Will be strange here too, curious and remote
As those beyond your hour may think of you.

I see deserted shores round Africa
White and too hot to touch, and from this softness
I pray to God that you have found your peace.

Words blunder, fall wide and noisily, for you
Whose life was so unclumsy, whose mind gracious.
We live here with the decencies of an age
That mute the words for praise and other passions
Along with crudity, or I would try
To shout a sonorous dirge for you, to reach
The birds that fly high over this thick air
For them to carry to Africa; even so,
There it would wither to a fruitless whisper
Burnt sterile by the holocausting sun.

Smooth saying and rigged rhyme, though, could never reach you
Sleeping at peace among the angels now
That you believed in once but not again –
Not angels like the bright swift birds, but powers
Great and unyielding, holding at their back
All that killed you, keeping you safe within.

The hot sun watched you and the sharp sparse grass
Whom liquid chirruping above mossed earth
Should have surrounded in an April aura
Bearing you sweetly to your station now,
Not nervous cackling of African grasshoppers.
The sun destroyed you in its aiming eye,
The dry hard land, and cruelty of men
One to another. If any are sorry now
If there are any wish your death undone
Let them not spoil innocence or kill beauty.
Let them not do this to another one.

. . . . . . . . . . . . . . . .

How arrogant we are who think we know
What you would have liked best. The soft green earth
That is my choice was nothing to you then.
Had it been so all forms and colours that pleased you
Had held you by the choice with which they beckoned,
As worthless flame held Moses' eye and saved him.
And you would be alive to say with us
'Even if I hate it, it is beautiful;
Man will do so, although I die for it'.

Though green or sand; sea-shore or suburb road;
Africa, England; love or unconcern
Are so much nothing to you that to say so
Is quite irrelevant, we babble here:
We cannot understand a silence where
None of our thoughts matter. That is to live,
However miserably – and we are living.
With absolute power, like a helpless baby
Fixed on its need without all fear or favour
You have left, whom neither the bright earth nor hope
Could comfort from extremity. We now
Mundane, recovering, distractable,
Need all the comfort that you could not take
For the wind howls here and peace is far.

# BLACK DOG MELANCHOLY

O black beast, you have got me now
Your foul red mouth breathed all around my face;
Through all the years of hunting, tracked me down,
Loping slowly, your quarry was so sure.
O many pleasant mornings you've let me have
Believing that upon this eminence
Or out in cliffside wind I had escaped you,
Thinking the fog would shift, and the light pour in,
Thinking, as animal, you could be matched.
And soothing still the evenings by the fire,
Still the blackbird unbelievable.
But now I know you near and do not move:
It is broad day and sunny, yet your shadow
Stands on my chest and covers all the land.
There is no lost neglected little corner
You do not know, and you have got me now.
Black rabid dog, there is no turning
No byway you could miss me while I lay low,
Black stifling dog, why do your eyes glare so?

## RECIDIVISM

The gulls are making a great clamour
To get me out,
Screeching from outside my window like a farmyard aroused.
'Come on come on come on' this huge beast on the roof yells
continuously.
His brothers are wheeling delicately over the sea.

And up and out I would go, but on my way through the kitchen
The cosy apparatus of order holds out its arms.
House walls like ramparts built to keep out weather
Allow one to see flowers in pots and smell the sea
But keep away the probability
Of being weakened by the stench of one more hope
Crushed: a body lacerated so disgustingly
Turning to poison between the granite wall and the sea.

## HIGH DEVIL, DEEP PIT

There is a fearsome path in the West country
An edge of rock joining two promontories
That stick into air, not sea, but as unnourishing
As crags that are washed by salt.

Lovers' Leap, some call it, or the Devil's Tightrope.
They are two lovers preserved in their hour of peril
Forever joined and riven, by impassable need.
One got across, they say, the other fell
Meat for his pursuers, yet they found
Barren rocks only strewn on all that ground;
And she turned stone through mourning.

Even to-day when a feat of engineering
Has pushed a road along the crevasse bottom
Bringing cars and teas, and a telephone
In case of emergency in a freak June storm
I should not care to be here after dark,
Nor linger even in Summer daylight, when
The blunt-winged buzzards wheel, knowing their land
As high above me as I above the gully.

There is, among the scratchy crags, a patch
Of close green turf away on the other side.
Did freedom lure the lovers, or the call
Of voices strummed from unearthly rocks by the wind?

Oh dizzy Devil pleasure who shall cross?
Between the gulfs of pleasure on the one hand
And heights of misery to the seaward side
I edge and slither clutching at thin roots.
Would it be better to be trapped below
Turned into stone in a desert whence none can fall?

## A METEOROLOGY

The wind has been blowing from the Sahara
And dropped Summer on us.
The desert that sucks up all green, spitting out only dust,
Has scattered strange buds on our pavements;
Mitigated through mountain passes packed with snow,
Filtered through grey seas,
The stare of the furnace has produced shadowy windflowers,
And little pale stems in our moist woods.

The fierce moment shrivels up thought
Like hay in a brick oven – a puff of ash,
As the melted core a hand that wants it now
Leaving a black shrunk object, like banana skin in the sand.

The steel is tempered to a salad bowl:
We hold it and offer it, full of green sap;
Fanned through dispersing passages, tunnels
Burrowing into time, the ruinous moment
Might open out to life like these wax beauteous
Magnolias, holding their lush cool cones in the air.

## ROSE IN THE AFTERNOON

Not rose of death:
Drawing in to your centre each wave of colour
That your arrested petals give to the air –
Dying inwardly the petals do not fall.

Nor rose of heaven:
Calm at the centre of this city
Monstrous moons, exuberance of stars
Have nothing to do with the light that you collect.
The light of the world has nourished your cut bloom
Drop by drop drawn down into your blood
As drop by drop your root took life from the ground.

Far down the river a cork popples the water
The motion quivers and rocks the air until
Rose in my room you catch and turn the movement
Mote by mote absorbed into your flesh
The vibrant morning tide within your veins.
Equally, hands moving in shuttered clubs
Though no light enters there to give time progress,
Flick flash-ringed fingers as red five black queen
Fall. Seeping through streets this gleam feeds you.

Day by day you calcify, embalming
The vigour you exhale. Fragile you have
Subdued the molten morning in your calyx
The palpitating golden fire that poured
Over the ridges of buildings, right angles, volutes;
And converted percussion of day to this calm strong flowing
Light lapping gentle round the afternoon;
Will equally subdue the night to come –
A ray shooting the dark – into a mere
Closure of a known twilight, not different state.

O rose in the afternoon, your only movement
The imperceptible falling in your blood,
Your vibrant stillness more speaking than all the voices,
If I could give you as answer, my sentence your statement
I would be dumb in peace with the light gone
And only your image waking in the dark.